Let Freedom Ring

Benedict Arnold

by Susan R. Gregson

Consultant:
Lt. Gen. Dave R. Palmer (U.S. Army, Retired)
Superintendent, U.S. Military Academy, 1986–1991
West Point, New York

Bridgestone Books
an imprint of Capstone Press
Mankato, Minnesota

Bridgestone Books are published by Capstone Press
151 Good Counsel Drive • P.O. Box 669 • Mankato, Minnesota 56002
http://www.capstone-press.com

Printed in the United States of America

Library of Congress Cataloging-in-Publication Data
Gregson, Susan R.
    Benedict Arnold / by Susan R. Gregson.
        p.cm. — (Let freedom ring)
    Includes bibliographical references and index.
    ISBN 0-7368-1032-3
    1. Arnold, Benedict, 1741–1801—Juvenile literature. 2. American Loyalists—
Biography—Juvenile literature. 3. Generals—United States—Biography—Juvenile
literature. 4. United States—Continental army—Biography—Juvenile literature.
5. United States—History—Revolution, 1775–1783—Biography—Juvenile literature.
[1. Arnold, Benedict, 1741–1801. 2. American loyalists. 3. Generals. 4. United
States—History—Revolution, 1775–1783—Biography.] I. Title. II. Series.
    E278.A7 G74 2002
    973.3′82′092—dc21   2001000131
                                              CIP

Summary: Follows the rise and fall of Benedict Arnold, America's most famous
traitor. Traces Arnold's life from his wealthy, upper-class childhood to his betrayal of
the American Continental army during the Revolutionary War. Explains Arnold's
legacy in our society today.

Editorial Credits
Charles Pederson, editor; Kia Bielke, designer; Stacey Field, production designer; Deirdre Barton, photo researcher

Photo Credits
Stock Montage, cover; North Wind Picture Archive, 5, 14, 17 (top), 21, 22, 25, 27, 29, 33, 34, 41; Library of
Congress, 7, 38; Mark E. Gibson/Visuals Unlimited, 10; Corbis, 11, 30, 37; Historic VU/Visuals Unlimited, 12;
Hulton Getty Collection, 17 (bottom); John D. Cunningham/Visuals Unlimited, 18; American Civil War Vol. 3/
Corbis, 42

1   2   3   4   5   6   07   06   05   04   03   02

Table of Contents

1   Hero to Traitor   4

2   Young Benedict   8

3   Hero   16

4   Traitor   26

5   Later Years   36

6   Benedict Today   40

Features

Map: The 13 American Colonies   9

Timeline   42

Glossary   44

For Further Reading   45

Places of Interest   46

Internet Sites   47

Index   48

Chapter One

Hero to Traitor

During the Revolutionary War (1775–1783), Benedict Arnold was known as "the bravest of the brave." He was a fierce and brilliant military leader who inspired his men. He captured a heavily armed fort without firing a shot. He forged through a wild Maine winter to attack the Canadian city of Québec. He created a small navy on the shores of Lake Champlain in New York. There, he boldly led a bloody battle against much larger British warships.

Benedict's soldiers later defeated the shocked British troops, who had to retreat and surrender. Without that victory, America likely would have lost the Revolutionary War. If Benedict had died then, we might know him today as a great American hero.

Many people considered Benedict Arnold to be one of America's best army officers.

"Blessed" Benedict?

The name *Benedict* comes from a Latin word meaning "blessed." Benedict's family felt it was important for sons to carry the name of their fathers before them. Benedict was the fifth in his family with that name. He named his son Benedict, who became the sixth. For years after Benedict's treason, many Americans would not name their sons Benedict. They did not want their sons to carry the name of a man who had turned against his country.

But he did not die, and later, a single event overshadowed Benedict's heroism. This courageous American officer betrayed the American cause. He later wrote that he acted out of "love to my Country." But he did not expect the world to judge his actions as he saw them.

More than 200 years later, Benedict's expectation has proven true. His name does not mean hero, as it might have. "Benedict Arnold" means only one thing: traitor.

On Board the Vulture Sepr. 25th
1780

Sir

The Heart which is Conscious of its Own rectitude, Cannot attempt to palleate a Step, which the World may Censure as wrong; I have ever acted from a Principle of Love to my Country, since the Commencement of the present unhappy Contest between Great Britain and the Colonies, the Same principle of Love to my Country Actuates my present Conduct, however it may appear Inconsistent to the World? who very seldom J[udge of] any Mans Actions.

I have no[t] myself, I have too often ex[...]

In this letter to George Washington, Benedict gave reasons for his actions. He said the world "may seldom judge right of any man's actions."

Chapter Two

Young Benedict

Benedict Arnold was born during the winter of 1741 in Norwich, Connecticut. Connecticut was one of the original 13 American colonies that fell under British rule.

Benedict's father was a successful businessman, and the Arnold family was well respected. As a wealthy young man, Benedict attended private school away from home. He was a daring boy who thought up many wild adventures.

By the time Benedict was a teenager, his father's business had failed. There was no more money for private school, and Benedict returned home. While he had been away, two of his sisters had died from disease. Only one sister, Hannah, was left.

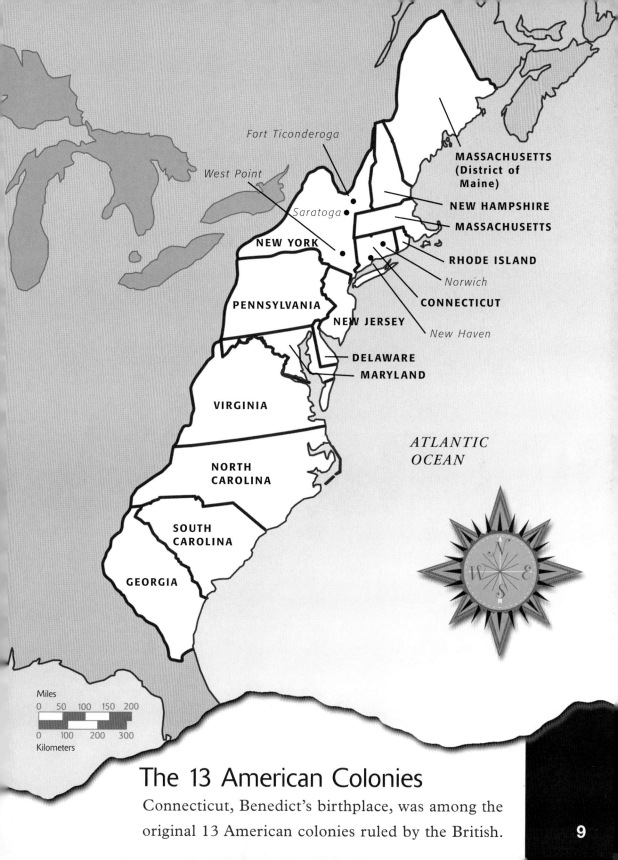

Fort Ticonderoga

West Point

Saratoga

NEW YORK

MASSACHUSETTS
(District of
Maine)

NEW HAMPSHIRE

MASSACHUSETTS

RHODE ISLAND

Norwich

CONNECTICUT

New Haven

PENNSYLVANIA

NEW JERSEY

DELAWARE

MARYLAND

VIRGINIA

ATLANTIC
OCEAN

NORTH
CAROLINA

SOUTH
CAROLINA

GEORGIA

Miles
0   50 100 150 200

0   100   200   300
Kilometers

The 13 American Colonies

Connecticut, Benedict's birthplace, was among the
original 13 American colonies ruled by the British.

After the family business failed, Benedict's father began to drink heavily. Benedict's mother relied on Benedict to bring his father home from places where he had been drinking.

Other teenagers insulted Benedict's father. Benedict's temper was hot, and he fought these boys. He was fearless, and his bold manner rubbed people the wrong way. Benedict's temper, courage, and confidence played a large role in his later life.

The Lathrop brothers became rich running an apothecary shop that might have looked like this one.

Apprentice

Benedict's life of ease ended. He planned to work as an apprentice, learning a skilled trade. In the 1700s, an apprentice often lived with a master craftsman. This person taught, fed, and supported the apprentice. In return, the apprentice did whatever chores the master assigned.

When he turned 14, Benedict became an apprentice to his mother's cousins, Daniel and Joshua Lathrop. The Lathrop brothers owned a nearby apothecary shop, which was like today's drugstores. The Lathrop shop carried wines, fabrics, ingredients for medicines, and other items.

Benedict saw the Lathrops' wealth and wanted the same success. The brothers lived in large houses with servants. Their homes contained expensive furniture. Benedict worked hard to learn the apothecary trade. His skill at math made him valuable to the business.

Apothecary Cabinet

Business and Marriage

By age 21, Benedict's apprenticeship ended. With support from the Lathrops, he opened his own shop in New Haven, Connecticut, where he sold medicines and books.

At first, Benedict's shop was successful. He dressed like a wealthy businessman and traveled to London, England, to buy the best products for his store. But he often was slow to pay for them. This pattern of spending and being in debt followed him all his life.

Benedict owned a fleet of trading ships that helped make him rich.

Benedict also had to pay his father's debts. He sold the family home in Norwich and brought his sister, Hannah, to New Haven to manage the shop. He then turned to trading to make more money.

Benedict bought a fleet of ships. He learned to sail them and went on long trading voyages to the the West Indies. These islands lie south of America. Benedict also traveled to Canada to buy goods to sell in America.

In those days, colonists could buy only British products. Traders like Benedict wanted to sell goods that colonists could not get from Britain. He brought certain items into the colonies illegally and then resold them. Many traders smuggled like this in colonial times to make more money and to avoid paying British taxes.

By this time, Benedict had fallen in love with Margaret Mansfield. The couple married and soon had three sons. Benedict often wrote to Margaret from his sea voyages, begging her for news. But there was no regular mail service, so her rare replies often did not reach Benedict for months.

Problems with Britain

Meanwhile, people in the American colonies were becoming angry with the British government. And the American Tories and Whigs disagreed about what action to take.

Tories were colonists who supported British rule. They sometimes were called Loyalists because they were loyal to the British government. Benedict

Benedict's militia wore uniforms that probably looked like these.

and other colonists were Whigs, or Patriots, who believed America should be independent of Britain. Benedict felt British taxes were hurting his business. He worried that the colonists were giving up their freedoms.

Patriots began to form militias. These groups of men volunteered to fight for their rights. Each colony had its own militia. In 1774, Benedict became a captain in the Connecticut militia. Like many other militia leaders, he often used his own money to pay for supplies, food, and weapons. Benedict's militia practiced with weapons, marched, and wore colorful uniforms. Benedict saw war ahead, and he wanted to be ready.

The French and Indian War

From 1754 to 1763, Britain and its American colonies fought France and Canada in the French and Indian War. When Britain won the war, Canada became another British colony. The British government wanted to raise American taxes to help pay for the expensive war. Most Americans felt they had already done enough by helping the British gain Canada.

Chapter Three

Hero

In 1775, the British commander in Boston, Massachusetts, Thomas Gage, received orders to capture weapons stored in the countryside. Gage's soldiers left Boston on a warm spring day. They headed toward the Massachusetts towns of Lexington and Concord.

At Lexington, local militiamen tried to stop these Redcoats, the world's best soldiers. A British officer ordered the Patriots to lay down their weapons, but someone fired a gun. Suddenly, gunshots, smoke, and shouts filled the air. Eight Patriots were killed and 10 were wounded during this first battle of the Revolutionary War. One British officer received a leg wound.

British Redcoats and
American militiamen
fired the first shots of
the Revolutionary War
at Lexington,
Massachusetts.

The British Redcoats marched on to Concord. There they captured some weapons and started to return to Boston. The Patriots, however, had heard about Lexington. As the British marched, the colonists gathered to fight. They attacked from woods, fields, houses, and barns. Overpowered, the Redcoats ran. In all, more than 250 British soldiers were killed or wounded. The Patriots had 94 dead, wounded, or missing.

British soldiers were nicknamed Redcoats because they wore bright red uniforms.

Benedict traveled to Concord with his militia but arrived too late to fight. He asked the Massachusetts Patriot leaders for permission to capture Fort Ticonderoga in New York. This well-armed British fort had ammunition and weapons, which the Patriots badly needed. The Massachusetts leaders hesitated, since an attack on the fort would be an open sign of war. They finally gave Benedict some money, ammunition, horses, and permission to gather militia members.

The Fall of Ticonderoga

On the way to New York, Benedict met another Patriot named Ethan Allen. He was leading his own group to attack Fort Ticonderoga. The two men argued about who should lead the attack and finally agreed to lead together.

The militia attacked Fort Ticonderoga at night. The group crept into the fort. Benedict and Allen woke the British commander and demanded his surrender. The attack was such a surprise that not a shot was fired. The commander surrendered the fort.

Benedict stayed in New York to run Fort Ticonderoga. He received a higher rank, but in a month, another officer arrived to replace him. Benedict was upset about being replaced. Angry, he left the fort and headed home with his men.

Back in Connecticut, he learned that his wife had died. His sister, Hannah, was caring for his three sons and running the business. Benedict rested at home for several weeks.

At summer's end, Benedict met with George Washington, the commander of the new colonial army. Washington recognized Benedict's bravery and military excellence. Benedict proposed leading an army through Maine into Canada to attack the city of Québec. Washington agreed, and Benedict left that autumn with more than 1,100 men.

Winter in the Wilderness

Autumn turned to winter, and the trip through Maine turned harsh. Rain, snow, and floods slowed the army, which ran out of food. Almost half of Benedict's men died on the journey. Finally, the exhausted men met Richard Montgomery, an American general who had just captured Montreal.

Benedict and Montgomery joined forces to attack Québec on New Year's Eve. The British overpowered the weakened colonists. Montgomery was killed immediately. Benedict was shot in the leg. He tried to direct his soldiers while propping himself against a wall, his leg bleeding. He eventually collapsed, and the attack fell apart. The Americans left Québec but waited all winter outside the city.

Benedict and his men attacked Québec during a snowstorm on New Year's Eve, 1775.

By the spring of 1776, British soldiers had arrived in Québec from Britain. Benedict's leg wound had mended. He and his army retreated to Lake Champlain in New York. These waters along the Canadian border provided a natural barrier that could keep the British from entering New York. Benedict realized that the area needed to be protected.

Benedict boldly led an army across Maine to attack Québec.

The Battle of Valcour Island

The British decided to invade New York across Lake Champlain. First, they had to take apart some of their ships and move them to the lake.

American forces in the area had only a few small ships and guns. Benedict feverishly worked all summer to build a small fleet on the lakeshore. His experience with his own fleet of ships helped him train his soldiers how to sail.

By summer's end, the British had prepared more than 30 ships. Benedict's ships were ready, too. The Americans hid behind tiny Valcour Island, halfway across the lake, and surprised the British. After heavy fighting, Benedict's fleet was almost trapped. But during a foggy night, Benedict's ships escaped, chased by the British.

On shore, Benedict destroyed his remaining ships so the British could not capture them. His small band of survivors made it to Fort Ticonderoga. By then, winter was arriving, so the British decided to wait until spring to continue attacking. Benedict had not won at Valcour Island. Yet the battle gave the American army time to prepare for the British invasion.

A weary Benedict expected praise for his action on Lake Champlain, but the praise lasted only a short time. Five officers with less experience than Benedict were promoted. He felt insulted and threatened to resign from the military. Washington begged Benedict not to leave, and he was finally promoted to major general. But Benedict felt the recognition for his efforts had come too late.

The Tide Turns at Saratoga

Benedict did not leave the army. By autumn of 1777, he was back in battle, this time at Saratoga, New York. His commanding officer, General Horatio Gates, was cautious. Benedict wanted to rush into battle. Gates called Benedict arrogant. Benedict called Gates weak.

Gates ordered his soldiers only to defend the American line at Saratoga. Benedict disobeyed and led fierce attacks against the British. A bullet hit him in the same leg that had been wounded at Québec. Benedict's efforts succeeded, and the British surrendered. Gates was angry and possibly jealous of Benedict's success. He ignored Benedict's central role in the victory. Other people felt differently. One of Benedict's soldiers wrote that Benedict was "the very genius of war."

The victory at Saratoga was probably the most important of the Revolutionary War. It boosted American spirits and convinced the French that the American army could beat the British. Soon the French, whose help the Americans badly needed, would fight alongside the Patriots.

Though his leg was wounded, Benedict led Patriot forces to victory at Saratoga.

Chapter Four

Traitor

Benedict's leg took months to heal. Doctors wanted to cut it off, but Benedict would not let them. He wondered if he would ever fight again.

Benedict finally returned to his hometown of New Haven, where people treated him like a hero. Washington encouraged Benedict to visit military headquarters in Valley Forge, Pennsylvania, when he felt better. Washington wanted to give Benedict his next assignment.

Shifting Loyalties

Benedict arrived in Valley Forge weary and badly limping. Washington was afraid Benedict could not lead troops in battle. The British army, however, had left Philadelphia, and the American army was taking over. Washington suggested that Benedict become Philadelphia's military commander. Benedict agreed.

Philadelphia was a bustling city when Benedict took over as military commander.

In June 1778, Benedict and his troops arrived in Philadelphia to cheering crowds. But Philadelphia's citizens were deeply divided. Disagreements ran deep between the city's Whigs and Tories.

As military commander, Benedict had much influence. He hosted large, expensive parties at his home. He entertained rich Philadelphians, many of whom were Tories. Benedict began to date Peggy Shippen. Peggy had many Tory friends and sided with them.

Benedict Goes on Trial

The Patriots were unhappy that Benedict had so many Tory friends. They soon accused Benedict of misusing his position. They said he closed shops in the city, resold the goods, and kept the money. Benedict was outraged. He resigned as Philadelphia's military commander and requested a military trial called a court-martial.

Months passed as angry Whigs gathered evidence against Benedict. At the court-martial, most charges were dropped. Washington was instructed to scold Benedict, who felt mistreated and unappreciated.

Turning Traitor

While awaiting trial, Benedict married Peggy. He loved his new wife, and eventually her Tory feelings influenced him.

Peggy Shippen married Benedict when she was a teenager. Here, Peggy holds one of their children.

West Point Then and Now

West Point is located high on a bluff overlooking the Hudson River. This location allowed the Patriots to stop enemy ships trying to sail past. The colonists dragged a heavy chain across the river to control traffic. Ships had to slow down and turn to avoid the chain. The stalled ships were an easier target for the guns at the fort.

Today, West Point is a famous military academy where young men and women earn a college education. They then serve America as officers in the army. A memorial at the college honors the American generals of the Revolutionary War. Benedict's name is not on the memorial.

West Point Military Academy

Peggy knew a British army officer named John André, who worked closely with the British commander. André directed some British spies, who watched American troop movements and gathered information about American plans. Benedict sent André a letter saying he wanted to join the British army as a general.

For months, Benedict and General Henry Clinton, the British commander, exchanged letters in secret code. Benedict made it clear that he wanted money to fight for the British. To prove he was serious, Benedict sent Clinton information on American troops. He even sent information about Washington's movements.

Meanwhile, Washington missed Benedict. He had no idea that Benedict was secretly talking with the British. He trusted Benedict and wanted his advice. He quietly urged Benedict not to leave the army, even after his court-martial.

Benedict asked Washington for command of the American fort at West Point, New York. This request from a general who enjoyed the challenge of battle surprised Washington, but he granted the request.

West Point guarded the Hudson River. The fort was important in keeping the British from cutting the colonies in half. Washington himself called it the "key to America." Benedict believed that surrendering the fort to the British would cripple the American army and end the war.

Try Writing a Code

Spies during the Revolutionary War used secret codes to disguise the meaning of their letters. These codes, or ciphers, often were based on well-known books.

Instead of writing a word in the letter, the spy wrote down a page, line, and word number from the book. For example, spies might use a popular encyclopedia for their code. The numbers "256.8.10" might mean "Look at page 256, line 8 on the page, word 10 in the line." Benedict wrote to British officer John André in this way.

Try to write a message to a friend using a cipher. Be sure your friend knows which book you are using to write the code. You might try a dictionary or even a school textbook you both use.

The Game Is Up

General Clinton promised Benedict 20,000 British pounds (about $1 million today). In return, Benedict agreed to give West Point to the British. He gathered the plans to West Point and arranged to meet André, who traveled from New York City by ship. André went ashore in an area swarming with both Loyalists and Patriots. Fearing capture, André was not happy about the arrangement. Benedict insisted that André would be safe.

The two men met at a house that later was called "Treason House." There, André took the plans for West Point and hid them in his stocking. The ship that had carried André to West Point left while he was ashore. He was forced to return to New York City by land. He traveled out of uniform to avoid being recognized as a British soldier.

Three Patriots captured John André, who offered them money in exchange for his release.

What Do You Think?

Benedict escaped from West Point on a British ship called the *Vulture*. Thomas Paine, a well-known Patriot, wrote that one vulture received another. What do you think Paine meant?

On the way, three Patriots captured André. He showed them a pass that Benedict had given him. The men were not convinced that André was a Patriot. They searched him and found documents in Benedict's handwriting. André offered the men money to release him. Instead, they brought André to local militia leaders, who finally realized a plot was under way. The militia sent copies of the documents to Washington.

Washington received the copies when he arrived at West Point for breakfast with Benedict.

Just before Washington arrived, Benedict learned that André had been captured. The traitorous general dashed away, first by horse, then by boat. He safely reached the British ship that had brought André. Benedict escaped to New York City, but André was hanged as a spy.

Standing with the Enemy

Benedict believed that the British would properly recognize his abilities. The British made their new officer a brigadier general in charge of Loyalist troops. Benedict led his troops on fierce raids against fellow Americans in Virginia and Connecticut.

The fighting in Connecticut was especially terrible. During one raid, a group of Patriots tried to surrender. Instead of accepting the surrender, Benedict's Loyalists killed the men.

Watching from a distance, Benedict wondered aloud what the Patriots would do if they captured him now. It is said that a nearby soldier replied, "They'd cut off your wounded leg to save as a reminder of your bravery. Then, they'd hang the rest of you as a traitor."

Chapter Five

Later Years

In 1781, British General Charles Cornwallis surrendered his British troops at Yorktown, Virginia. It was a bitter defeat for the British army and signaled the beginning of the end of the Revolutionary War.

When the British army returned to Britain, many Loyalists left with them. Benedict and his family were among them. In London, the king and queen of Britain warmly accepted the family.

Benedict never received all the money that he had hoped to get for his treason. Years later, Benedict received about a third of what he wanted. He and Peggy also received a small yearly amount of money from the British government.

Benedict asked for an active command in the British military. He was refused. Soon his supporters lost control of the British government.

The end of the
Revolutionary War began
when Cornwallis
surrendered his British
army at Yorktown,
Virginia, in 1781.

Americans at the Peace Table

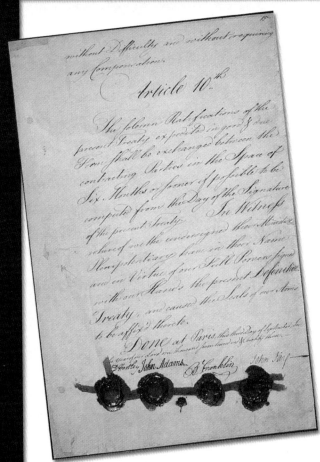

Treaty of Paris

Several Americans traveled to Paris, France, in 1782 to begin peace talks with the British. The men included Benjamin Franklin and a future American president, John Adams.

The Americans and British worked out a final treaty in 1783. This Treaty of Paris formally ended the Revolutionary War and recognized the United States as independent of Britain.

A Patriot-friendly Whig government took control and simply ignored Benedict. His family struggled with debt as they spent more than they had.

Back to Business

Benedict went back into business and moved to Canada, where his family later joined him. He built a ship for trading in the West Indies. The community liked Peggy but not Benedict. His reputation as a traitor had reached Canada.

Benedict did well in business at first. However, when he tried to collect loans he had made, he was accused of greed. Some townspeople burned an effigy, or likeness, of Benedict on his front lawn. In late 1791, he and his family sold their belongings and returned to London.

A Sorry Ending

Benedict continued to lose money and could not repay loans. During the last 10 years of his life, his leg was constantly painful, and he had a lung disease. Benedict died on June 14, 1801, at age 60. He was buried in a London graveyard following a little-noticed funeral.

Peggy Pays the Debts

After Benedict died, Peggy needed to pay his debts. Many of his business deals had fallen apart, so he had borrowed money. Peggy sold their house and most of their belongings. She also used money from investments in Philadelphia. Peggy died of cancer in 1804 at age 45.

Chapter Six

Benedict Today

Without Benedict, the colonists may not have won the Revolutionary War. He was admired as a champion of the Patriot cause.

What caused such a shocking turnaround in a man famous for his heroism? No one really knows. Maybe his family's poverty made him crave the money that betrayal promised. Maybe he needed to pay for an expensive lifestyle. Maybe he distrusted the French. Perhaps he did it for the reason he himself stated: love of country.

Whatever the reason, Benedict Arnold's battlefield bravery has passed from memory. But Benedict is not forgotten. He is remembered every time someone spits out the words "Benedict Arnold." This insult is Benedict's reputation.

Hundreds of years later, it still reaches beyond his unmarked grave in a London cemetery.

It is not clear why Benedict betrayed his country. There may have been many reasons.

TIMELINE

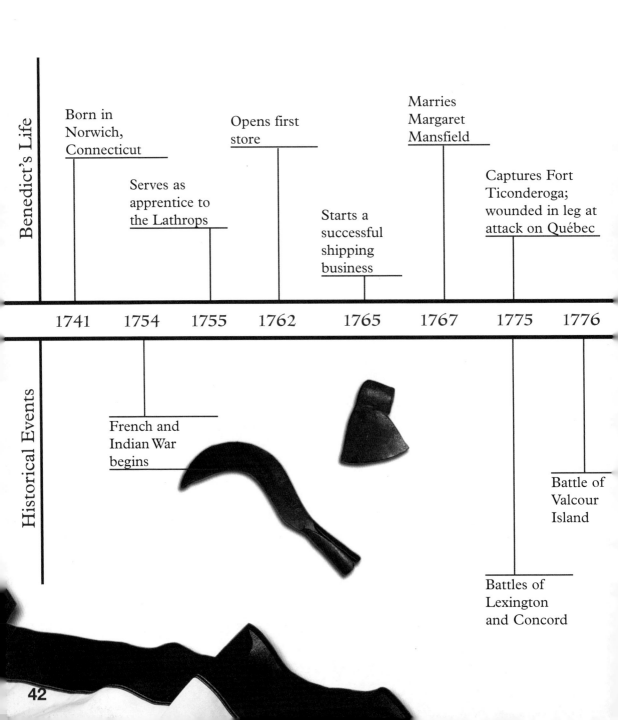

Benedict's Life

Born in Norwich, Connecticut

Serves as apprentice to the Lathrops

Opens first store

Starts a successful shipping business

Marries Margaret Mansfield

Captures Fort Ticonderoga; wounded in leg at attack on Québec

| 1741 | 1754 | 1755 | 1762 | 1765 | 1767 | 1775 | 1776 |

Historical Events

French and Indian War begins

Battles of Lexington and Concord

Battle of Valcour Island

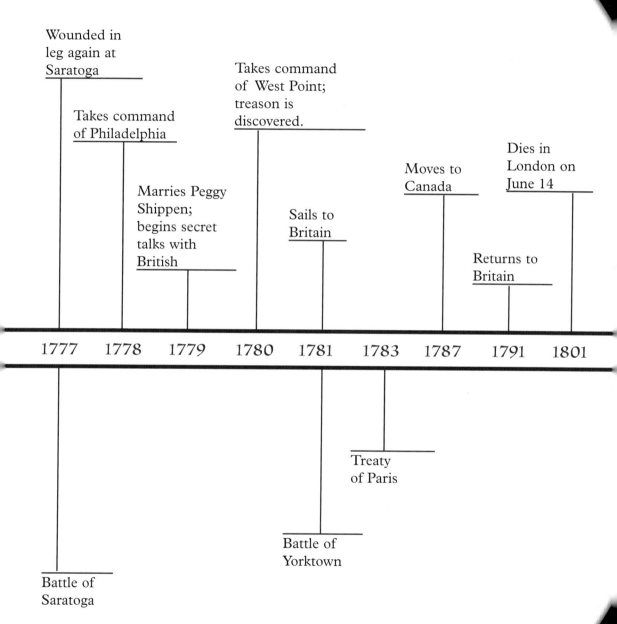

Wounded in
leg again at
Saratoga

Takes command
of Philadelphia

Marries Peggy
Shippen;
begins secret
talks with
British

Takes command
of West Point;
treason is
discovered.

Sails to
Britain

Moves to
Canada

Dies in
London on
June 14

Returns to
Britain

1777   1778   1779   1780   1781   1783   1787   1791   1801

Battle of
Saratoga

Battle of
Yorktown

Treaty
of Paris

Glossary

apothecary (uh-POTH-uh-ka-ree)—a store that sells medicines

apprentice (uh-PREN-tiss)—a young person who lives with and learns a skill from someone who already has the skill

Loyalist (LOI-uh-list)—someone who supported British rule in the American colonies during the Revolutionary War

militia (muh-LISH-uh)—a group of citizens who fight during emergencies

Patriot (PAY-tree-uht)—a person who sided with the colonies during the Revolutionary War

Redcoat (RED-koht)—a British soldier during the Revolutionary War; the name came from the bright red coats the soldiers wore.

Tory (TOR-ree)—a person who sided with Britain during the Revolutionary War

traitor (TRAY-tuhr)—someone who turns against his or her country

treason (TREE-zuhn)—acting against a country to which loyalty is owed

West Indies (WEST IN-deez)—a group of islands that lie in waters south of America

Whig (WIG)—a person who sided with the American colonies' fight for freedom from Britain

For Further Reading

Fritz, Jean. *Traitor: The Case of Benedict Arnold.* New York: Putnam and Grosset, 1997.

King, David C. *Benedict Arnold and the American Revolution.* Woodbridge, Conn.: Blackbirch, 1999.

Lutz, Norma Jean. *Benedict Arnold: Traitor to the Cause.* Philadelphia: Chelsea House, 2000.

Thoennes Keller, Kristin. *George Washington.* Let Freedom Ring. Mankato, Minn.: Bridgestone Books, 2002.

Todd, Anne. *The Revolutionary War.* America Goes to War. Mankato, Minn.: Capstone Books, 2000.

Places of Interest

Fairmont Park

Benjamin Franklin Parkway and
26th Street
Philadelphia, PA 19130
Historic mansions, including the
one Benedict and Peggy Arnold
lived in after their marriage

New Haven Colony Historical Society

114 Whitney Avenue
New Haven, CT 06510
Large collection of Benedict
Arnold information and letters

Old Burying Ground

Norwich, Connecticut
Benedict's family headstones;
missing are the headstones of
Benedict's father and older
brother Benedict Arnold, who
died in infancy; historians believe
that angry townspeople destroyed
the headstones in 1780.

Saratoga National Historical Park

Stillwater, NY 12170
Displays the "boot monument" to
Benedict and his injured leg

U.S. Military Academy

West Point, NY 10996
Oldest continuously occupied
military post in the United States
and home to Benedict's treason

Westchester County Historical Society

299 Saw Mill River Road
Elmsford, NY 10523
Richard Maass Collection on
Benedict and John André

Internet Sites

The Battle of Lake Champlain
http://odur.let.rug.nl/~usa/E/champlain/champxx.htm
History of Valcour Island

Lake Champlain and Lake George Historical Site
www.historiclakes.org
Information and photos of the area around Valcour Island

Spy Letters of the American Revolution
University of Michigan, Clements Library
www.si.umich.edu/spies
Stories of spies and their methods during the American Revolution

Thinkquest
The Revolutionary War: A Journey Towards Freedom
http://library.thinkquest.org/10966/data/barnold.shtml
Biography of Benedict

U.S. Military Academy at West Point
A Brief History
www.usma.edu/PublicAffairs/history
An overview of West Point, the object of Benedict's treason

Index

Adams, John, 38
Allen, Ethan, 19
André, John, 30, 32–35
Arnold, Hannah, 8, 13, 20

Canada, 4, 13, 15, 20–22, 39
Champlain, Lake, 4, 22, 23–24
Clinton, Henry, 31, 32
codes, 31–32
colonies, 8, 9, 13, 14, 15
Concord, Massachusetts, 16, 18, 19
Cornwallis, Charles, 36

France, 15, 25, 38
Franklin, Benjamin, 38
French and Indian War, 15

Gage, Thomas, 16
Gates, Horatio, 24

Hudson River, 30, 31

Lathrop, Daniel and Joshua, 11, 12
Lexington, Massachusetts, 16, 18
Loyalists, 14, 32, 35, 36

Maine, 20
Mansfield, Margaret, 13, 20
militia, 15, 16, 19, 34
Montgomery, Richard, 20–21
Montreal, Canada, 20

New Haven, Connecticut, 12, 13, 26
New York City, 32, 33, 35

New York (state), 4, 19, 20, 22, 23, 24
Norwich, Connecticut, 8, 13

Paine, Thomas, 34
Patriots, 15, 16, 18, 19, 25, 28, 30, 32–34,
    35, 40
Philadelphia, Pennsylvania, 26, 28, 39

Québec (city), Canada, 4, 20–22, 24

Redcoats, 16, 17, 18
Revolutionary War, 4, 16, 25, 30, 32, 36,
    38, 40

Saratoga, Battle of, 24–25
Shippen, Peggy, 28, 29–30, 36, 39
smuggling, 13
spies, 30, 32

Ticonderoga, Fort, 19, 20, 23
Tories, 14, 28
Treason House, 33
Treaty of Paris, 38

Valcour Island, Battle of, 23–24
Valley Forge, Pennsylvania, 26
Vulture, the, 34

Washington, George, 20, 24, 26, 28, 31,
    34–35
West Point, New York, 30, 31, 32, 33, 34
Whigs, 14–15, 28, 38

Yorktown, Virginia, 36